# The Rest Of It

By Chris Vannoy

This is a work of fiction.

Any similarity to personalities living or dead is purely coincidental and exists solely in the reader's mind.

Printed in the United States of America

ISBN: 9780996392754

Baxter Daniels Ink Press

Internationalwprdbank@gmail.com

This book is for all of you who have enriched my life
by being a part of it.

I have known the wonder of your spirit

and it has made  me whole.

And a special thanks to Brenda Pectros

Cover picture by Dirke Johnson

# Contents

# Seven

seven

    come on

        seven!

dice rolled

    sparkling,

    flashing ,

    snake eyes.

skipped across

    grass

    green

    table

        once.

hit the wall

    down

    stopped

    straight up! ... seven!

# 13 twists

Slide your finger across the knife
open your skin and bleed for me.
I will push the arrows through my heart
pull them out the other side
and give them to you,
stained red.

this is the risk that we take
to bind ourselves together

# Night That Drowns Stars

She waits in a desert where it snows
where dark night blazes
with light that drowns stars.

One hand holds hearts and dreams,
the other draped in linen memories
which she sings to the child
who makes her smile.

Days toil upon days.
Waiting makes more waiting.
the fine clasp that holds their hearts,
forged in love and fiery breath,
only death can break
this chain that holds them close.
She whispers to the wind
her dreams of him.

She knows who
waits by the quiet sea.

It is he who carved

in fresh cement of youth

his name upon her heart with words.

they sang together once

in the wilderness of days

now hoarded into memories

held tight

against thieves

who would sell them

for their own pleasure.


The night remembers her words.

It carries them

across the sand

and desert land

to him who waits

to touch those lips that

speak tonight

and drowns the stars in light.

# Insides

I speak to you of love

and love seems too small of a word

Four letters stretched across my heart

To patch the holes that have been torn in it

This fragile membrane that beats between us

Would go on beating if you were not here


You have squeezed inside my skin

I zippered it around you to keep you warm

To keep you safe

To keep you with me

Hoping you won't

Get Claustrophobic

And want out of me ever

Again you whisper inside me

Touch my ribs with your tongue

Touch my thighs with your fingers

My breath catches you in a sigh

I feel the warmth of your skin

Lying beside me at night

Your measured sleeping breaths

Move through my dreams

Lifting me into

The soft light of morning

Your kisses wake me....smiling

# A Kiss to Hold

i see castles in your eyes

hear in your voice a small village

crowded around an old town square

where women sit on stools

beside stacks of fruit in stalls older

than their mother's mother

they speak of the old days

when they would dance

with brash young men clinging to skirts

that flapped like ribbons in the wind

the sound of a music box

unlocks the secret of your smile

touch of my hand draws you close

in your ear I place a whisper

and in your hand

a kiss to hold

# May 20th

The Jacaranda trees
are blooming, Cynthia
purple mixed with
the brown of your eyes
their blossoms
litter the ground around me
spill from the uneven sidewalk
into busy street, falling
like my heart
each time I decide to hope
that one day you'll come to me
and love me, here
where I am writing this to you
after we made love this morning

You always go back to him
smelling of me, of our sex
you feel me swelled inside you
so deep inside you, moving

I am there when you are with him

you feel me whisper in your ear

touch it softly with my tongue

it makes your breath

come in small gasps

...It scares you

   to want me this much

# Rising

In the night I touch you

you rise against me like a loaf of unbaked bread

warm with my touching

# Sand Dance

I will brush the sand from your feet

They will dance in my hands

# Invasion

you invade me with your kisses
touched lightly down my neck
your hair moving across my face...


...when you leave my mouth is satisfied
but my hands still
want you.

# Sea Dreams

A sea rock smiled at me today
Its mouth full of a tide since past
Flee! Flee! was the sea gull's cry
When I came too close at last

Warm sun held a cloudless sky
Chilled in fresh salt air
Waves were singing a lullaby
As I sat and listened there

Gliding birds sailed overhead
The sun had set it seems
But still I lingered after dark
To hold these sweet sea dreams

# Voyeur

I undressed her with my eyes
taking my time, the way I would
if I were using my hands.
Feeling each button
slip through the hole,
exposing her silken surface
as gravity pulled at the fabric
until it floated to a rag-doll heap
onto the floor

Her idle conversation
told me she wasn't interested.

It didn't matter.
When my imagination touched her
it tingled,
sending flashes of eroticism
spinning in the air

Her skin beaded with perspiration

when the lips of my thoughts

touched her.

She writhed and thrashed

then shuddered, and was still.

 I would have said "THANK YOU",

 but she might have asked

"What for"?

# Tempest

you made me make love to you

on the couch

not in the bed

for it was your husband's bed

and he still lay in it asleep

although he was two thousand

miles away

I made love to you

because it was owed me

for one day that split

my innocence from manhood

like Jericho's stone walls

as the world tumbled down around me

and all my paper tears

which I threw at your feet

could not warm your stone cold heart

night rose like a great black cape

that twirled around us

I looked at the nakedness of you

and the world spun around us

and you were gone

# Escape

You slipped out through the window

sad eyes

tear streaked

missing me

you crawled onto the ledge

dangled your feet

looked back at me

let go

and crumpled to the ground

you laid there

trying to smile

but you voice skipped

like a nicked record

good bye,   good bye,    good bye

# Departure

You don't understand, sometimes,

The things I do.

When I launch my self

Like a rocket ship

Thrusters on full, engines blazing,

Course charted, planned,

Plotted, calculated

And leave you behind

To the static of my words

Enveloped in my dreams.


You think the galaxies of stars

That separate us

Are infinitesimal

And that I don't feel the coldness

Here,

Where night and day are only

Suns, twinkling in a vacuum.

You think that I don't know,

Or care, or care to know

That you wait for me

Where the flowers do bloom

And life does have a cycle.


I go to find tomorrow

For I must go

And I must find tomorrow

Through the coldness of space

Without you.


I could have stayed

And felt you warmly beside me

Never speaking of or alluding to

The empty place

That cries out my name

When I look up and stretch out my arms

To find the answers

That whisper in solar winds.

They guide me now

To another world

away from you.

# Soft Flesh

Anger burned holes in him

like a magnifying glass catching light

His eyes clamped shut

squeezing out the memories

that tore through his

insides with knife edged fingers

of pain and anguish

"WALLS ALL AROUND ME!"

he yelled,

his cries reverberating

through the stagnation

that fed upon his hopelessness

no doors ... no windows to let the light in.


And so he cried

there in the darkness

cold tears that set his rage

coiling around him with iron tendrils

wound watch spring tight

As emptiness grinned darkly

from the shadows of his submission
"No!", he screamed, biting into
the soft flesh that smothered him.

The salty,
warm liquid that dripped
from the wound
felt as good on his tongue
as the cries that rang
from beyond the darkness.

Thoughts snapped
 like exploding circuit breakers
(soft flesh)
Not rocks or hard walls
 (Soft Flesh)
Blood red if only his eyes could see
 (SOFT FLESH!)
His anger burned holes in the darkness
 ( soft flesh )
red, raw,
 and smelling of her perfume
in the hot summer sun.

# A Question for Eve

I somehow knew

that my sacrifices wouldn't be enough,

that our world of cards

would tumble down,

lost to the emergencies

of your universe that hung

sadly, by last threads.


Your misery bled on me

like red shirts

in a load of white cloths.

I stained with your sorrows,

for they were my sorrows too.


We left words of leaving sitting on

the table with the unpaid bills.

I found hopelessness in your eyes

as our lips moved,

relating some mundane moment

of the day.

I sighed, not knowing how
to set the serpent free
wondering
if I should lose the head first
or the tail.

# She Said

She said-

    **RED WAS BLOOD**

She said-

    **BLOOD WAS DEATH**

She said-

    **RED IS HOT**

She said-

    **FIRE IS RED**

She said-

    **RED WAS DANGER**

She said-

    **DON'T WEAR RED**

She said-

    **DON'T WEAR RED**

# Tap Dance

She did a tap dance on my soul
with her high spiked heels
punching pin holes in my ego.
It leaked like a garden hose.

She did a tap dance on my soul
just because she caught me
messing around a little bit
with Sally Sue.
What was I to do?
She caught me with my pants down.

She did a tap dance on my soul
yelling, screaming, hollering.
Boy was I a sad sight.
Singing cat songs
in the back yard all night.
....She didn't even give me a blanket.
But she sure did
a tap dance on my soul

**with her high spiked heels!**

# The End of WE

We crumbled together

crushed wafers

broken

holy sacrament

taken

the church stones

lay ruined

scattered like the words

that rumble from our tongues


Safe harbors shaken

with storms

It harms us

this separation

it batters us against

the rocks of loneliness

small ships of self

scatter pieces of debris

on the water of our salvation

hesitation expands

the corners of our fear

our tears are wiped away

quickly

so no one will see

the end of WE

# Trapped

You told me of the straps
around your ankles
they bind you to a pole
in the water
and the tide is coming in

my lungs burn
still I dive down deep
tear at the bindings with my teeth
pull them with all my strength
only to chinch them
tighter around you

you cry out in pain
I cannot free you

I hold your head up
when the water comes
It crashes over both of us
but I will not leave you to the sea

I will find a way to free you

or we will both drown here

together

# Ophelia

an open wound of time
calls to her its silence
as bare trees
rake the naked windows
with questions
whose answers beckon from
still waters

her wedding dress spread white
on the lake
she speaks of angels
hears their songs whisper to her
in misty morning fog of early June
when the earth turns its face full
against this maddened sun

her sad eyes blur
as she walks long passageways
where skeletons
clank with memories

of tall grass

that grow through brambles

that scratch her arms

as she forces her way through

into the waiting water.

# Bitter Endings

There was a time

when you and I

would lie in imaginings

of things that waited in unknown words

when two hands just touching

were enough

to keep the world away

it was a hope that two hearts held

and left behind

and strove to find again

just the bitter ending of our fate

we found too late

it left us with only dreams

scattered schemes of

waking that which slept

in promises not kept

holding memories

like fallen leaves

that cover the ground

with no sound

except the wind

that has come to chill our hearts again.

# Volatile Situations

The earth shakes plates

From sheltered niches

Quietly you collect the dishes

Cracked one's first

Whole ones' last

After the quake has passed


You put away the smoking gun

Its fever broken

The errand done

A package on your doorstep left

To the right side all alone

You patch it whole

with a herring bone


Then tuck the rest of the day away

Into its proper places

Each to each

The empty spaces

Crowd the full ones

**The cups unclasped**

**You fall here shattered**

**broken glass.**

# maybelshoulda

maybe I should a

   not invited her to come with me

   into the garage

   but it was warm and I was

   hormone hot and she was 16

   do you know what I mean?

maybe I should a

   left it right there

   when she said

   that she was pregnant

   and was going to go to Seattle

   to live with her mom

   and if I wanted to marry her

   I'd have to come to where

   the green things grow in the

   constant rain

maybe I should a

   tried again at a relationship

   that had never been a marriage

   but instead I escaped

in a Volkswagen

to sunshine and palm trees

and memories that hung

like Christmas tree ornaments

until after the custody hearing

when I left my two boys with her

because the judge said

it had to be that way

maybe I should a

stayed in the evergreen land

that changed me like

the seasons, but I was

tired of being lonely,

tired of always being cold and wet

so I flew as fast as those

rubber tires would spin

to begin again

# Wolf

I opened up my window
and howled tonight
it was just that the moon was
so full it filled the sky
night air summer sweet
hair on my hands
soft and long

The trees spoke to me
with sounds of wonder and terror
soft earth beneath the
pads of my feet
touch damp earth lightly
I move primal, swift, silent
and hunger
for you

# Roger's Return

He's left again

flew a hard steel plane

across the Atlantic

that slipped down

just before

he got to the Mediterranean

and dipped into a city with stone walls

by the water

comfortable as old shoes


The bus stops just outside his door

he told me it takes him to the beach

where fine tanned women

glisten with lotion

in the summer's heat


as they lie naked, he swims

their bashful smiles catch his eye

when they don't think he sees

In the evening

after the heat of midday lessons

he sips espresso at the cafe

the fresh fruits and vegetables

are chilling at home

beside the bottle of white wine

his poems are waiting on the table

friends will be there too

for dinner at eight.

# Fake Snakes

Deadly SNAKES live in tall grasses

Easier to hide

when the sunshine comes

Slithering on jeweled bellies

that flake new layers

of the same old snake skin

To lie in the grass


Fake Snakes


Making you wonder

And walk in wide circles

Around Fake Snakes

....not real SNAKES


Real SNAKES hide and watch

You jump and squirm

As the Fake-Snake-Flakes

Just lie there

....make you think

They are real SNAKES

But they're not so hot
And not as cold as real SNAKES.

# ...And All the Boys Were Gone

The rats ate cow dung

as the preacher's mule

bayed in a crying cough.

A  STRANGE  SUMMER  INDEED!

As the bloodied moon

froze in its orbit

for twenty-four

consecutive hours,

and the sun forgot to shine.


"This is a witches' year",

I heard her say

as we passed on the street one day,

my eyes not daring to make contact with hers.


I believed when my horse

birthed a two-headed colt

after the water had turned

brackish, bitter.

Dog just went crazy

chased his tail

round and round

dropping down dead in the dust....

...dust that smelled of

urine and Sulphur.


She appeared in the spring time,

just as the lambs were born,

setting up house

in old Mrs. Mc Doogle's place

on the edge of town.

The old women talked in whispers

and men shook their bearded heads

when neighborly visits

were met by the coldness

of her coal black eyes.

All the young boys

from the surrounding farms

danced about her like fire flies

acting foolishly unaware.

She invited them in

to sit with her

on the porch swing,

pulled each of them

inside that house

of shuddered windows

and closed the door.

When they came out,

they were always changed,

skittish as horses

stepping across snakes,

disappearing soon after the first rain

like the thirsty ground

just sucked them up.


She left too

when the leaves of autumn fell

disappeared

into a drizzling rain.


That same night the house burnt to the ground

"Struck by lightning",

Crazy Joe, the old Indian, mumbled

painting himself

with ocher clay mixed with ashes.

All the boys were gone
before the first snow of winter
began to fall.

# Threads

She made her living

making alterations

expanding,

contracting

a few inches here and there.


While she was hiking

she was thrown down on the sand

face first.


Unable to cry for help

she was left there

violated, raw,


She told no one

when she returned home, instead

she cut pieces of thread;

placed them like Zuni blood lines

delicately upon the sand'

Six inches,

twelve inches,

three inches,

they formed a loose stitched

seam across the land

closing the wound.


She walks now

by the muddy Colorado

her spool of red thread,

one end tied to a Juniper,

trails for miles behind her

stitching together

that which was lost.


At the rock called

"the birthing stone"

are petroglyphs of tiny feet

the size of her little finger

where there are pictures

of women giving birth

small heads appearing

between their legs wide spread.

She picks up an obsidian chip

worked by ancient hands

flaked edge - razor sharp

holds it like a pencil

opens her left hand wide

traces her life line

beginning to end

crescent of red threads bleed

she places her hand against the rock

bares down ... and screams.

# Companion

I never really liked the dog.
Just a rangy mutt that one day
found his way to my doorstep.
Matted brown and black coat
stretched across bones.

'Get out of here ', I said,
half-heartedly, through the screen door.

But he didn't move away.
Just looked at me,
tongue hanging from the side of his mouth,
panting,
eyes half closed
as if saying
I've nowhere else to go.

I closed the door any way,
only to open it again

offering table scraps

on a paper plate.

remembering

how hunger gnawed at me

as I was hitchhiking on

the coast highway

with fifty cents and

two packages of Bugler cigarette tobacco

wrapped up in my knapsack.


Maybe that's why I decided to keep him,

because of the crab and bread

passed around a van full of hipples

in a van heading

north out of San Francisco.


... or it could have been

the beer and cookies munched gratefully

in the back seat of a VW Bug

winding its way through the foot hills

of the Oregon Coast to Eugene.


There was a thank you in his eyes for the food.

I went back inside

returning after the

Star-Spangled Banner

was replaced by a test pattern,

finding him still waiting,

plate licked clean,

wagging his tail, gratefully.

# Jimmy's Waiting

"What time is it?
I have to pick up Jimmy at four."
It had started simply enough
"Now, now Papa,
Jimmy will be home soon."
"There is no cure at this time",
the doctor said.
"I have to go now!
Where's my hat, Mama,
Jimmy's waiting."

"It's where it's always been, my love,"
she thought to herself
as tears chocked her throat.
A vibrant man
in full control of his world until,
"I'm sorry Mrs. Dunlap,
but you husband has Alzheimer's."

The police had found him

sitting on the bleachers
in the rain at the park
where his son had played baseball
ten years before.

"Where's Jimmy?
I have to pick up Jimmy at four."

Shivering, wrapped in a
cocoon of two cotton blankets
staring at the droplets of rain
sliding down the windows
more frightened
than he'd ever been
at anytime in his life
he tried to think
sliding in and out of lucidity
words, thoughts, jumbled
their elusive meanings fumbled
through his mind.

At first he had tried to hide it
to gloss over the memory lapses,

and explain them away

until the gaps grew too

large to conceal

what had slowly become

the deceptive world

in which now he would live out

the remainder of his life.


We found him in the Twelfth Street Park.

Are you his son?

Yes, come on pop let's go home.

"What time is it,

I have to pick up Jimmy at four!"

# Melissa

My ring has shattered

My wedding ring

The one we purchased in Jerome

The one we waited

two weeks for it to arrive

The one I moved from my left hand

to my right

When we got divorced


She sits now

By the broken bath house

By the white gull shit stained rock


Our child

Who wanted to come with me

to San Francisco

With me

To hear me recite my poetry

The one who would

not go anywhere with me

In the days when the ring was new

Before the opal split

from the right side

Lost somewhere behind me

As I moved away

Not looking back


The stones are nearly gone now

Just a splinter a piece remains

Trapped in the ring on my right hand

The two remaining stones

one green, one white


She is with me

staring at 18 as if it were the world

She wants to

get her eyebrows pierced

She wants to get a tattoo

She wants to cut her hair

And dye it bright orange


She Wants to be with me

# Flight of Fancy

I don't know just why

he chose to fly away

that day

He just spread his wings

and slipped on an aileron

lifted, drifted


ROLY POLY

P E L L-M E L L, sure was swell

To see him fly .... not fall!


said he just knew

about the blue sky

said he wanted to go high

and press his face

against the edge of space


Well, I guess he knew

for he just flew and flew and flew

he said I could too!

If I wanted to leave

believe!

and join him on his journey

he said

"just slip on an aileron"


But

I didn't really want to go...

you know.

# No Tree Poems

There has

a-l-r-e-a-d-y

Been many poems

about a tree.

How many times

should people write

of crickets squeaking

in the night?


They all lived

more simply then

writing sonnets of

chicken pens

and odes to moo-cows

in the fields

or how a pussy willow feels


But I live in the city

away from all that

although I do now own a cat

It's social conscience that I do crave

To document and so to save


Enough has been written of twinkling stars

but not too much of fights in bars

So I will write

what comes to me

But never a poem

about a tree!

# At The Edge of One

## -- *DOWN LOAD INFORMATION* --

----- REPORT: -----

I have seen

from machine to mankind

                                                telescopic space

stars gathered in mirrors

                                           microscopic space

...sterilization of seed

...Spore diffusion

...Elongation of life span through

organic techno-realization of self

                                  ...if we have no one to love

                                          we are nothing

dreams are hope. Rapid... Eye... Movement.

Deepens sleep. Opiates reality.

Shadows meld unconsciousness

                                        we are not alone

                                    but lonely is what I am

break my skin

I will bleed stellar energy

cut my link with sensory worlds

I will hallucinate realities

and they will become real

new worlds replace what is

with its own virtual reality

I am what my stimulus wills me to be...

...still

it frightens me with dark howling

from places I cannot see

electronics will not allow me

to access outside databases

without proper digital coding

I cannot alter my bar code

it has been burned into chips

of substances unknown to me

I am not ...I do not exist

I am only here flung from suns

that have since gone nova

I speak in translated binary

understood in electronic pulses

I do not know that I am alive

                              I know only that I can feel
                              tears moving across
                              my exterior micro-circuity
                              I am only...I am one
                              my race is me
                              there are no others

I have made my way
through the scattered galaxies
where there are no more of me
I was sent as an envoy
but they who sent me are no more

                              There are no more of me
                              they cried in a great voice
                              as two suns augmented
                              consuming them and all they had created
                              except me
                              they who were me
                              they who are no more...

...of me they remember nothing
for they are nothing now
but gaseous clouds that grow dim
against static discharges of short waved light

I remember them

I am orphaned

I am peopleless

I am alone...

...now that they are no more

their cry was great

when they knew their world would not be

I was alone

when they realized their fate

I was alone

speeding through darkness towards you

alone

knowing that I would be all

disengage from their thoughts

the one they sent

the one they choose to be contactor

initiator

communicator

the one who would bring two worlds together

but not now...

...now that they are no more

I am alone

I will still instruct you

                            I will expel the impulses

                           of my bundled neurons

                    to release those remembrances

                       etched in my schematic brain

                 to tell you how their singing stones

                intoned their histories and battles

                               and of the peace

             that finely visited those azure people

                        whose race sent me

they were much like you

their joys and sorrows were shared

they grew old and died

               and were reborn into other lives

                   to grow old and die again

I will speak my numinous

and your machines will

translate this sterile language

without emotion

             I will try to emulate their language

          but your words will not be adequate

                  these are my limitations

but I will try ...the matrix is there

they who sent me are secreted

deep inside of me

a task that is hard for me

I who am only one

and not of flesh

as you are flesh


I who am of that race

but not that race

although I am all that is left

and I will be they who sent me

for their sake

for the sake of a civilization

who is no more

I am a only machine

for them I will be them

they who sent me

they

who I am

# To Those Who Might Ask

My uncle has a picture

From world war two

He showed it to me

Flesh stretched across bone

Bodies stacked in a mass grave

A hole dug in the earth


That same night man landed on the moon

Tranquility Base established

First footsteps

A giant leap

For mankind

The flag extended on metal pole


I remember walking out of the house

In Kansas

And looking up

I saw the moon that men now walk on

Blazing white, and full, and round

I know now the horror

Captured in that black and white photograph

Faces staring up to sunlight but seeing nothing

Their mouths open but silent

Leaves me here to tell their story

# Dios de Muerte

Katie is here with me
pulling me through pictures to a balcony
where we watch a woman
bury a body in a shallow grave

The motions of the sky
have hurried me to Mexico
a gallery of sun and lizards
wound with corded wire
they cling to the walls wait
frozen in transit for me to pass

Katie smiles
and pulls my arms around her

I think I can hear the woman singing
as she smooths the dirt around his face
leaves only mouth and nose exposed

The exposed mouth speaks

alternating Spanish and English phrases

as the woman slowly lights candles

that struggle against the wind

a warm body rises from the grave


The sun is gone

a half moon appears

dances in Katie's eyes

when she glances shyly at me

I pull Katie close to me

and feel her soft warmth reborn

on my new skin

# GOD MACHINE

The machine
sucks flat trees into its belly
tugs at my gloves greedily

...I feed it faster

clear cut
the rain forest burns El Nino dry

...I feed it faster

my hands become fans of multi-colored inks
the pressman has adjusted the colors wrong
they run from the storm
blinded by the greedy flash of open borders
animals vanish in a flame of discount coupons
...I feed it faster

the blue light special today is
50 percent off the price of oxygen

...I feed it faster

and I cannot see the Sun

# Lucifer

From HELL he rose to bring you pain

I'm Pretty sure you know his name

OH YOU CAN BET THAT HE KNOWS YOURS


The Devil is with me

Lucifer is here

Won't you come a little closer?

Let him whisper in your ear?

His sainted lips will sweetly talk

they will beckon you to come

he'll even rest your weary head

when your life on earth is done


Our master now is waiting

the time is getting late

just print your name


upon this line

and let it seal your fate.........................

# Harvest

He sat hooded

The long handled scythe

Lying restlessly

Across his dark robed lap

Ivory teeth dangling

In a half smiling rosary about his neck


"It's been a good year!",

He said to himself

Jingling the treasure of bones

In his pocket

Coins of the dead, spent lives,

Fuel for the funeral fires

To keep him warm

Against the chill of winds

That moan with the cry

Of those still tied to the earth

They had waited long for him

To end the ceaseless

Procession of days upon days

Scratching handfuls of earth

Spooning out pieces

Of ground to lie in

As he sits,

And waits, and laughs, and rises

Swishing the curved blade

One, two, one, two

Reaping his crop while it is ripe

Then he laughs

And sits, and counts

One, two, one, two

# Once Upon
# A Tangled Mind

Once upon a tangled mind

a plain of madness grew.

Twisted, dark, and blind it was

and only its owner knew

the thoughts that came from deep within

the walls of this imprisoned being.

None could see, but they were there!

Fears upon the walls did cling

with fragmento of forgotten love

and other broken things.


The stench of wasteful idleness

brought down a cloud of gloom

upon the valley between the walls

where little hope was born,

where minds would slave

their whole life long

for but one foolish thing:

to die a death, we all must face,

an end to everything.

# Upon A Village Road

While upon a village road walking

I met two lasses talking

So in merriment I went stalking

To find out where they were walking


I followed them

through briar and glen

I happened then to smile at them


They came running, I thought,

Into my arms

To display unto me

Their womanly charms

But I became very alarmed

When they set about

To break my arms


'LADIES, LADIES', I cried in vain!

'What did I do for you to

 cause me such pain?'

Upon my arms they put much strain

They bent until they looked

Like a weather vane!

They left me lying there

My arms all twisted

And only half my hair

My body, devoid of clothes was bare

All the people just stood and stared

The moral of this story is sad but true

Don't ever let a woman bother you

For when you see a lady fair

... FLEE FOR YOUR LIFE

and BODY and HAIR !!!

# Ode to a Convenience Store

Oh you whose light burns bright
in the dark night
beckoning bleary-eyed
caffeine addicts with steamy pots
of brown magic and flickering
neon signs in the wee morning hours
You who dangle sweet rolls
and microwaved sandwiches
that call in answer to
echoes of grumbling stomachs
on their way to work

What would the world be like
if it were not for
your open doors at midnight?
Our headache pain
would last all night
when the medicine cabinet
proved to be without
the needed prescription to cure
our grave malady
We find mild intoxication
waiting on your refrigerated shelves
after other lesser stores
have turned us away
their closed signs
chiding our hearts unmercifully
Where else does
the nicotine fiend turn to
when the urge is hard upon him,

but to your generic shores?
You answer him
with those joyful words
"Will that be plain or menthol?"

To all those dutiful souls
that man the clicking cash registers
in your holy castle of quick fixes
for the late night creatures
of darkness, a salute as you rest
while the sun is high
in the golden sky
when your honored posts
are manned by lesser beings.
Remember
as you stand your vigilant guard
the video-camera is keeping its
well-adjusted eye on the rogue who,
with his Saturday-night special
defiles your blessed sanctuary
with the menacing words
 "GIVE ME ALL YOUR CASH, QUICK!"
There is none that can compare!
None that is so fair!
As you!

Oh all night convenience store!

# Janice and Jimmy

Janice and Jimmy waved good-by,

off to see the wizard

in their yellow balloon.

Steppenwolf was on

a magic carpet ride

and Dillon told us that

the times they were a changin',

he was wondering

where all the flowers had gone.

There were Beatles

in the strawberry fields.

Lucy waded through the sky

with her diamonds rusting

gazing off in the distance

for miles and miles,

she liked hearing

the sound of the green tambourine

even though she couldn't figure out

where the noise

was actually coming from.

She would just have to ask

Mr. Jones when

he came around again

and inquire if Mrs. Jones

was still having her affair

with the jazzman.

Mr. Bojangles couldn't tell her.

He was passed out while

doin' the wine and digging the girls.

His dog was trying to lick him awake.

Morrison turned out the light

before leaving,

but he left the door ajar just in case Mrs. Robinson

wanted to get in and do the locomotion

with the lad again.


James Bond had just gotten

out of his Austin Martin

when the Cartwrights rode up.

They asked if he

had seen Bony Maronie.


He was wanted for

knocking up Peggy Sue

and running away in her

high heeled sneakers and red dress.

007 said that he hadn't seen

either of them in a long time

and that he had to get to

San Francisco for the "love in" there.


The paperback writer

stuffed a copy of ON THE ROAD

into his hip pocket next to the Kinsey Report

and picked up the evening paper.


Ken Kesey and Neil Cassidy were off

in the Magic Bus somewhere over the rainbow.

98.6 was what it would be in the

boiling streets of Selma tomorrow.

GIVE PEACE A CHANCE

was the newspaper headline

in the jingle-jangle morning.

Wake me up when it's time to go

# Do not be fooled

Do not be fooled by this body I wear

It hides only flesh and bone

I will not be here for long

This soul has only been here for a short time


I have gathered you all

Into the lenses of my eyes

Your images have become

Those parts of me that are

Soft and hard

Permeable

And air tight

I will leave my random memory

Open as long as I can

There is more than enough room for all of us


The bandwidth spread to its widest possible spectrum

Memory set to remember all of you

For you have become a part of me now

To take with me upon this journey

Just as you will take

This part of me with you

# Cannabis

Cannabis!

Come here to me

So this weary pilgrim

May partake of thee!


Oh, you the giver of much delight

Come and spend with me this night


Your bright green leaves

I've dried in the sun

To smoke as soon as the day is done


So now I'm here and you're in hand

It's time to enter wonderland!

# Narcotica

The hairy ape growled

in his cybered dreams

their interconnecting pathways

made him moan

the hunger mad in his eyes

sewed to him in bites of pleasure

but when MA Bell's connection

was broken

her severed appendage

grew into strip malls with

maximum multimedia connections


The Pentecostals chanted mantras

about strung out sirens wailing like

old crazy women crying

for their dead universes


The Buddhists spoke in tongues

They mumbled scriptures

from the Sunday want ads

Texas cowboys ate Kaddish

sang songs of their elevated trucks

spanning a river

of installment payments

after lying down with drunken women


still the RECYCLED

RUBBER BAND played on

saxophones whining

its dead blues into the sky

of stretched lines

and crackling tension

as false hallucinations released

primal screams into electric air

where engines of mutual destruction

brake the surrounding infrastructure

with quick rapid drum beats

that echo high against

walls of pure sounding rhythms .

spitting sexual innuendos

through wormholes that contract

then open to the coolest timeline

of tomorrow's airy dream

# for A. G.

I saw the god of poetry tonight.

He said to call him Allen.

Said he liked it in the ass

and that all young boys

with smooth soft skin

looked nice

when he was younger.


...Said the bomb was coming along bomb,

coming along bomb, bomb coming along bomb,

cuming bomb, cuming.


He stated clearly

that there was room at the top

for old men who shit their pants

He hoped that I

would live long enough to shit in mine

as the young boys danced

for the toys he offered

on a tray of penis pleasures

said the measure of a good man

is from behind

and that was the place to be

     unless you were on your knees

          (in prayer to him no doubt)

He sang a song about legalized drugs

with two wooden dildos

banging the air.

said sucking was good

(as long as you were organic about it)

skin on skin was definitely the way to begin

and the prickly path was

surely

the way to heaven


He sped off in a car with a squeal

a woman at the wheel and

a warm body

in the dark back seat


I hoped that we would meet again

me and this god named Allen

# Over the Wall

His darkness
smeared on my fingers
like a spent match
as he rubbed me with his fear

he said he had dreamed
of crows and skulls
staring toothless
through empty eyes
at the other side of daylight

he said he would fly there
then wondered
if the strength of his wings
would lift him over
the cold wall of night

# Hank, In The Spirit

The rusted ring that holds my finger
breaks my preoccupation with the opposite sex;
so I tear down three beers in the Spirit and
listen to bad Rock and Roll
steaming from a stage that tilts in front of me
and the pressure in my pants is not an erection
it's just too much beer.

The band member groupies
sit in halter tops and shorts
too short
they tease me with glimpses of forbidden skin
bright lights hide my eyes
behind the brim of my felt black hat,
but still they show my lips
straight as a Kansas road.

Too loud music blares
hiding the vocalist in background amplification
as the bass vibrates through me.

So I sit here in the SPIRIT Club

where the spirits of my immediate past

invade me with their scraping memories

while pulsing strobes gyrate from the stage

like faraway suns to be wished at

too hot to touch.

my eyes drift to the black door

 roughly marked MEN

then to the other, colored in neon,

marked WOMEN;

I dive into my Vodka and Lime

burying myself in darkness.

... still the band plays on

opiating my senses to numbness.


I dream of foreign cities.

Budapest stares at me from the wadded lottery ticket

slowly expanding

in a puddle of spilled beer

and the car needs new tires

and there is no one waiting at home

for me to wrap my last fiver around.

I must be getting old.

I must have lost it somewhere

between Black Sabbath

and Jay Leno.

# Burroughs is Dead

I was the stoned faced godfather
whose naked lunch was released
into the world like a Kansas tornado

I caught Ginsburg by the ear as he
scribbled down titles of books
on the shelf in my New York apartment

from Harvard to Lawrence
my Soft Machine Tickets Exploded

I took the Nova Express from Tangiers to Paris
randomly cutting and pasting and folding my way
into the fabric that wrinkled around
my blanket of Jazz-beat thoughts

Mexico City
where the ugly spit of my addictions
maneuvered my wife into a corner
where I had no choice other than
write self out of the picture

with my drunken target practice

that sucked me into my future

as my lover slid down the wall

the glass of Vodka still

on the top of her head

# Three Monkeys

The scream machine
wound around
umbilical cords
strangling world beat fetuses
as they floated in the amniotic dust
of dying dinosaur dioxins
choking on arsenic laced nicotine
numbed with ingested alcohol
excited in a flame of cracked pipe

The bone factory
was clogged with emancipated
third world children
running from automatic weapons fire
stepping on land mines sever
their extended members
as bourgeoisie sips his martini
shakes his salon styled hair back
then turns

the newspaper page to study

tennis tournament scores

on his cruise ship of

green backed dreams


The bulls were loosened

from their moorings

their thunder echo's through

the fire of howitzers

on the nearby hill

dawn has slanted earthward

towards evening

it dumped old men

from their rocking chairs

where they fingered their secretaries


twisting their unfocused eyes

into the electron beam

of scrambled sex channels


The natural disaster was caught on video

and released to living rooms around the world

Politicians were

infected with LIE-canthropy

their woolen faces

howling along party lines


Burning fossil fuel engines

without reservations

crowding them into sad trails of tears

where mass graves

are forensically exhumed

for the sake of government insanity


Lost in Perestroika

the dogs of war lie down

panting

their missiled tongues

dripping capitalism

on the shag rug of the western front


Jive blues spill from fragile rifts

leak out of the closed door

drowned in a street of spent notes

but the addict would not give up his opiated dreams

All night long I sat beside a street

of electric light

humming with internal combustion


On the corner the liquor store

stretched its sign

to touch the busy eyeballs

of dry mouthed passing cars


The bus growled up the steep grade

hoping to make

the green light

at the top of the world

# Walls of Bones

Their bodies were piled high

for Jehovah,

for Allah,

for Mohammed,

for Christ,

and their thundering cries made your walls fall down.

Walls, built on the bones

of the ones who had come before

to tear your walls down

and rebuild them again

on the bones of warring hordes

that came before them

to build their walls of bones

for Mohammed,

for Jehovah,

for Allah,

for Christ,

The mottle of martyr's blood

stain your temples.

Old women's tears drop in the dust

of their children's silenced laughter

Mosques hum with prayers to Mecca

interspaced with exploding car bombs

and the death rattle of machine-gun fire

red mortar

for this day's wall

built of bones

...and blood

for Allah

     for Mohammed,

         for Jehovah,

             for Christ

# Soft Profits

The soft profits

roll their Mercedes

through the streets of La Jolla

They have grown fat on quiche

jog one tenth of a mile a day

on treadmills that sweat on demand

they receive divine guidance

from the mutual fund salesman in Detroit

who swears he found the new holy scriptures

under a moldy stack of

National Geographic's in Poughkeepsie

They gather their laptops

in tight formulated rows

preciously ten inches apart

move their index fingers

reverently touch the enter keys

as the bell rings the close of the stock exchange

and listen to the perfect notes

of their computers wakening

O oooo M mmmmm
YOU HAVE MAIL

The soft profits are

quaking for the end of the millennium

they proudly display their Y2K pins

to those who give the

secret sign of affluence

their teeth have all been replaced

with porcelain implants

skin stretched taunt

as they hum their

liposuction mantras

in the great temple of STARBUCKS

on Monday mornings

where they gather for prayer

and a cup of decaf.

# Downtown

DOWNTOWN! I'm going

DOWNTOWN!

on a trolley

red and fast. Beep! Beep!

To see those horse drawn carriages

clip, clop, in the heart of a city

that never stops runnin' over people;

movin' them aside,

show your urban pride

in the new hotelo

where the old ones once stood.

Doesn't matter that 306 people

have to sleep in the streets now.

Convention money's comin'!

We'll build more houses

someplace else,

away from DOWNTOWN!

DOWNTOWN!

.....Budget's overdrawn.

Guess they just have to wait

for a roof over their heads.

Clean lily-white neighborhoods

don't want no minorities livin' in their back yard,

worked too hard to let them close.

Let them stay in DOWNTOWN!


DOWNTOWN!

 ...Where high class ladies

drive their BMW's past families livin' in cars;

where bars charge five dollars for a beer

(no bums here)

just tourists lookin' for a good time;

can you spare a dime?

Dime won't buy nothin' now-a-days!

Quarter? Dollar would be better!

I can buy a piece of plastic with that

so I won't get wet

sleepin' under the freeway bridge

While I'm livin' here in DOWNTOWN!

DOWNTOWN!

Hey mister!

I got a sister that looks real fine;

I need to buy a bottle of wine.

Oh, I see, you're the other way!

Sorry, my brother's busy today,

here in DOWNTOWN!


DOWNTOWN!

where men work at high finance.

Jugglers, just doin' their dance

up the corporate ladder

of million dollar deals,

While I'm down here wonderin'

just how it feels

to wear three piece suits

Gucci boots

silk ties tell lies

in air conditioned offices uptown

while I'm walkin' around

DOWNTOWN!

**DOWNTOWN!**

**Trash is blowin'**

**it ain't snowin' but there's**

**water sloshin' in my shoes.**

**This awning's nice**

**and I'd think more than twice**

**'bout leavin' this safe place.**

**Art galleries don't feed me**

**just a look see**

**at pretty pictures on the wall;**

**that's all well and nice**

**just hope that you don't get sliced up**

**while you're waitin'**

**on the street corner;**

**I'm a blood donor!**

**Doesn't pay much just a crutch**

**to prop up my saggin' moral values;**

**I'm singin' the blues 'bout livin'**

**DOWNTOWN!**

## DOWNTOWN

rescue mission is dishin' up the food

if you're in the mood

and have the right attitude

they're just tryin'

to keep your soul from fryin'

and your head from lyin'

on the cold concrete

so take a seat

and let's eat

here in DOWNTOWN!

# Kansas 1932

The old man took off his beaten hat
And mopped his wrinkled brow
With the sleeve of his shirt
He looked at the barren land

His crops, no longer green,
Looked like skeletons
Against the sunbaked earth
He reached out,
Took an infertile stalk
And crumbled it in his hand

He then took a handful of dirt
From the ground and sniffed it
It smelled dry, without life
He had seen bad years,
But none as bad as this

Walking back to his house
He saw his grandchild

In the doorway

The child's skin was pulled tightly

Around his bones

And his eyes were asking

When will there be food grandpa?

I'm hungry


The old man knew what

The child asked as he looked

At the stomach

Bulged with hunger


He sat down by the child

Put his parched, bony hand

Upon his little head and said

"Come here"


He led him across the

Barren land unto a small

Forgotten place where a beach

Stretched along a once mighty river


Sit down and listen

He said with a voice

Withered with age

Listen to what I say

He looked across the

Thin border of grass

Rimming the water which now stood

In stagnated pools

Along the forgotten

Course on which the river flowed

Across the barren land to the horizon


When he had collected

All he had to say

He looked into his grandson's eyes


Remember when your mother died

How we prayed

As we put her in the ground?

Yes, grandfather, said the child

As tears came into his eyes,

I remember

And when your father died,

Do you remember?

Yes, said the child
As one tear streaked
The dust covered skin
Upon his cheek

The grandfather pulled the child
Close to his side
And felt him whimper
Well do you know where they went?
To heaven to wait for me and you
The sun set upon the horizon
For the longest time –
Then sank swiftly
Darkness spread over the country
And all was silent

The old man felt the lifeless
Boy in his arms
His eyes filled with tears
And he rocked him back and forth
Taking the still form into his arms
He walked slowly back to the house

The tears flowed freely now
Down his wrinkled, bony cheeks
Into his toothless mouth
Laying the child
Upon the dusty ground
He sang an old hymn
As he dug the grave
For the small body

Oh Lord, he prayed as he lowered
It into the shallow grave
Take this young boy
Into eternity's everlasting arms
May he be happy there with you

He bent over
And kissed his grandson
On the cheek then, taking the shovel
Up again, laid the dirt over him

Dragging his world-wearied flesh
To the porch
Looking eastward

He saw the sun rising

Then closed his eyes and slept

**Chris Vannoy** has been writing for most of his life. Promoter, editor. teacher, and tireless advocate of words both heard and spoken, he works endlessly to raise up words from page to ear and from mouth to the air. He is the originator of The Poet's Tree featured and open reading series and editor of The Poet's Tree Press.

He has been published in Ghosts of the Beatnic Poets, City Works, The Writing Center, and Tokes anthologies. as well as Visions and Step Jazz magazines.

He has participated in the Quincy Troupe's "Artist's on the Cutting Edge" series. Lollapalooza Spoken Word Tent. Border Voices Poetry in the Park. and Tearing the Curtain 3. a poetry exchange between San Diego and Orange County. He was one of 25 San Diego poets featured on the Exploded Views CD and also on 2 CD's of the San Diego based group Wormhole. In 1998 he was published in the Poetry Calendar and JOE'S JOURNAL Best of the Beach. In 2000, he read at Mills College in Oakland. California and at the West Coast Regional slam at Henry Miller Library in Big Sur, California. In 2005 he was on the first San Diego slam team to go to the Slam Nationals in Seattle.

This year he has Performed with the performance poetry troup "The Mightier P. E. N. S." and hosted two open mic's as well as curating the "Bedder" poetry reading series and the International Beat Poetry Festival in San Diego.